W9-DDM-401

PRESENTED TO

_____

ON THE OCCASION OF

_____

FROM

_____

DATE

_____

A LITTLE INSPIRATION

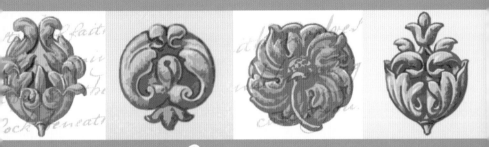

FOR A *faith* FILLED DAY

BARBOUR
PUBLISHING

DEDICATED TO MY *grandmother,*

MARGARET WILLIAMS STOKER,

WHOSE LIFE WAS AN EXAMPLE OF FAITH.

© 2003 by Barbour Publishing, Inc.

ISBN 1-59310-230-5

Compiled by Cynthia Margaret Stoker Franklin.

All Scripture quotations are taken from the King James Version of the Bible.

Published by Barbour Publishing, Inc., P.O. Box 719, Uhrichsville, Ohio 44683, www.barbourbooks.com

Our mission is to publish and distribute inspirational products offering exceptional value and biblical encouragement to the masses.

Member of the
Evangelical Christian
Publishers Association

Printed in China.
5 4 3 2 1

Faith is an action
based upon a belief
that is supported by confidence.

R. W. SCHAMBACH

Belief is truth held in the mind;
faith is a fire in the heart.

Joseph Fort Newton

Some things have to be
believed to be seen.

RALPH HODGSON

He does not believe that does not
live according to his belief.

THOMAS FULLER

The errors of faith are better than
the best thoughts of unbelief.

THOMAS RUSSELL

I could not say I believe. I know!
I have had the experience of being gripped by
something that is stronger than myself,
something that people call God.

CARL JUNG

I prefer a firm religious faith
to every other blessing.

HUMPHREY DAVY

The most valuable contribution
a parent can make to a child is to
instill in him or her
a genuine faith in Jesus Christ.

JAMES C. DOBSON

Many of us have inherited
great riches from our parents;
the bank account of personal faith
and family prayers.

NELS F. S. FERRÉ

A man of courage is
also full of faith.

CICERO

Whoever is happy will make others happy, too.
He who has courage and faith will
never perish in misery.

ANNE FRANK

When you come to the edge
of all the light you know
and are about ready to step off
into the darkness of the unknown,
faith is knowing one of two things will happen:
there will be something solid to stand on,
or you will be taught how to fly.

Faith is the bird that sings
while it is still dark.

PONSY

Faith walks simply, childlike,
between the darkness of human life
and the hope of what is to come.

CATHERINE DE HUECK DOHERTY

"Though He slay me, yet will I trust Him"—
this is the most sublime utterance of faith
in the whole Bible.

Oswald Chambers

I show you doubt
to prove that faith exists.

Robert Browning

Doubt your doubts,
not your beliefs.

JO PETTY

Apples of Gold

Faith is
a certain image of eternity.

JEREMY TAYLOR

Faith never knows where it is being led,
or it would not be faith.
True faith is content to travel
under sealed orders.

J. Oswald Sanders

Spiritual Manpower

Faith is two empty hands held open
to receive all of the Lord Jesus.

ALAN REDPATH

Victorious Christian Faith

Never be afraid to trust
an unknown future to a known God.

CORRIE TEN BOOM

Fear forces,
love leads,
faith follows.

KEITH MOORE

I see heaven's glories shine,
and faith shines equal,
arming me from fear.

EMILY BRONTË

Every tomorrow has two handles.
We can take hold of it with the handle of anxiety
or the handle of faith.

HENRY WARD BEECHER

That is, that I may be comforted
together with you by the mutual faith
both of you and me.

ROMANS 1:12

Faith in our associates is
part of our faith in God.

Faith makes the discords of the present
the harmonies of the future.

ROBERT COLLYER

If then God so clothe the grass,
which is to day in the field,
and to morrow is cast into the oven;
how much more will he clothe you,
O ye of little faith?

Faith expects from God
what is beyond all expectation.

ANDREW MURRAY

The essence of faith is
being satisfied with all that God is
for us in Jesus.

JOHN PIPER

The important thing is
not the size of your faith;
it is the One behind your faith.

ORAL ROBERTS

Faith does nothing of itself
but everything under God,
by God, and through God.

JOHN STOUGHTON

Faith that is sure of itself is not faith;
faith that is sure of God is
the only faith there is.

OSWALD CHAMBERS

It is not the greatness of faith
that moves mountains,
but faith in the greatness of the Lord.

JO PETTY

Apples of Gold

Seeds of faith are always with us;
sometimes it takes a crisis to nourish
and encourage their growth.

SUSAN L. TAYLOR

Take the first step in faith.
You don't have to see the whole staircase—
just take the first step.

MARTIN LUTHER KING JR.

Faith is building on what you know is here,
so you can reach what you know is there.

CULLEN HIGHTOWER

The secret behind getting more faith
is to get to know God more.

LESTER SUMRALL

Faith is our spiritual oxygen.
It not only keeps us alive in God
but enables us to grow stronger.

JOYCE LANDORF HEATHERLY
The Inheritance

The sweetest lesson I have learned in God's school
is to let the Lord choose for me.

DWIGHT L. MOODY

All I have seen teaches me
to trust the Creator
for all I have not seen.

RALPH WALDO EMERSON

Understanding is the wage of a lively faith,
and faith is the reward of an humble ignorance.

The experience of life nearly always works
toward the confirmation of faith.

THEODORE T. MUNGER

Life is a wilderness of
twists and turns
where faith is your only compass.

PAUL SANTAGUIDA

Faith is the first factor in
a life devoted to service.

MARY M. BETHUNE

I am one of those who would rather sink
with faith than swim without it.

STANLEY BALDWIN

Faith is like love;
it cannot be forced.

ARTHUR SCHOPENHAUER

Faith brings man to God;
love brings Him to men.

MARTIN LUTHER

Faith is not only a means of obeying,
but a principle act of obedience.

EDWARD YOUNG

The principle part of faith
is patience.

GEORGE MACDONALD

Prayer does not cause faith to work;
faith causes prayer to work.

GLORIA COPELAND

It is useless to pray for
more knowledge, power, or faith
until you begin to use what you have already.

HENRY BUCKLEW

Your Daily Spiritual Vitamins

Faithful servants have a way of knowing
answered prayers when they see it
and a way of not giving up when they don't.

MAX LUCADO

Faith, mighty faith, the promise sees
and looks to God alone,
laughs at impossibilities and cries,
"It shall be done."

CHARLES WESLEY

Nothing in life is more wonderful than faith,
the one great moving force which
we can neither weigh in the balance
nor test in the crucible.

Sir William Osler

Faith is not belief without proof,
but trust without reservation.

D. ELTON TRUEBLOOD

Things of God that are marvelous
are to be believed on a principle of faith,
not to be pried into by reason.

SAMUEL GREGORY

Faith begins where
reason sinks, exhausted.

ALBERT PIKE

Faith is believing in things
when common sense tells you not to.

GEORGE SEATON

I admire the serene assurance
of those who have
religious faith.

MARK TWAIN

Faith and works are as necessary to
our spiritual life as Christians as
soul and body are to our lives as men;
for faith is the soul of religion
and works of the body.

CHARLES CALEB COLTON

This is faith:
the renouncing of everything we are
apt to call our own and
relying wholly upon the blood,
righteousness, and intercession of Jesus.

JOHN NEWTON

Let us have faith
that right makes might.

ABRAHAM LINCOLN

For therein is the righteousness of God
revealed from faith to faith:
as it is written,
The just shall live by faith.

ROMANS 1:17

Faith is the gaze of a soul
upon a saving God.

A. W. TOZER

Faith is to believe, on the Word of God,
what we do not see,
and its reward is to see and enjoy what we believe.

I believe in Christianity as I believe in the sun;
not only because I see it,
but because by it I see everything else.

C. S. LEWIS

Faith is the radar that sees through the fog
the reality of things at a distance that
the human eye cannot see.

CORRIE TEN BOOM

Now faith is the substance of things hoped for,
the evidence of things not seen.

HEBREWS 11:1

Faith in an
all seeing and personal God
elevates the soul.

JUAN VALERA

The saddest thing that can befall a soul
is when it loses faith in God.

ALEXANDER SMITH

Little faith will bring your soul to heaven,
but great faith will bring heaven to your soul.

CHARLES H. SPURGEON

All the strength and force of man
comes from his faith in things unseen.

JAMES F. CLARKE

Under the influence of the blessed Spirit
faith produces holiness,
and holiness strengthens faith.

JUAN VALERA

Let us move forward with
strong and active faith.

More strongly have faith
and rejoice in Christ.

MARTIN LUTHER

The strength of the heart comes from
the soundness of the faith.

ARABIAN PROVERB

Every act in consequence to our faith,
strengthens faith.

ANNA LETITIA BARBAULD

God tries our faith
so that we may try
His faithfulness.

We can go through anything if we know
that Jesus is going with us.

OUR DAILY BREAD

Confirming the souls of the disciples,
and exhorting them to continue in the faith,
and that we must through much tribulation
enter into the kingdom of God.

ACTS 14:22

Faith is trust in what the spirit
has learned eons ago.

B. H. ROBERTS

Faith involves letting go
and knowing God will catch you.

CLERGY TALK

The steps of faith fall on the seeming void
but find the Rock beneath.

Faith is
necessary to victory.

WILLIAM HAZLITT

Keep the faith,
but not to yourself.

BREAD OF LIFE

Never yet did there exist a full faith
in the divine word which did not expand
the intellect while it purified the heart.

SAMUEL TAYLOR COLERIDGE

Faith is not a sense,
nor sight, nor reason,
but simply taking God at His word.

CHRISTMAS EVANS

A better world
shall emerge based on
faith and understanding.

DOUGLAS MACARTHUR

There was never found
in any age of the world
that which did so highly exalt
the public good
as the Christian faith.

FRANCIS BACON